THE SOUTHEAST DIVISION

BY JIM GIGLIOTTI AND ROBERT E. SCHNAKENBERG

Published in the United States of America by
The Child's World® • PO Box 326
Chanhassen, MN 55317-0326

800-599-READ • www.childsworld.com

ACKNOWLEDGEMENTS

The Child's World®: Mary Berendes,
Publishing Director

Editorial Directions, Inc.: E. Russell Primm, Editorial
Director and Line Editor; Katie Marsico, Managing
Editor; Caroline Wood, Editorial Assistant; Susan
Hindman, Copy Editor; John Barrett, Proofreader;
Tim Griffin, Indexer; Kevin Cunningham, Fact
Checker; James Buckley Jr. and Jim Gigliotti,
Photo Researches and Photo Selectors

Manuscript consulting and photo research by
Shoreline Publishing Group LLC.

The Design Lab: Kathleen Petelinsek,
Design and Page Production

Photos:
Henny Ray Abrams/AFP/Getty: 14
AP: 9
Brian Bahr/Getty: 24
Victor Baldizon/NBAE/Getty: 27
Bettmann/Corbis: 7, 8, 35
Chuck Burton/AP: Cover, 19
Peter Cosgrove/AP: 2, 32, 33
Scott Cunningham/NBAE/Getty: 15
Tim de Frisco/Allsport/Getty: 29
Tony Dejak/AP: 26
Greg Fiume/NBAE/Getty: 20
Focus on Sport/Getty: 10, 36, 45
Jesse D. Garrabrant/NBAE/Getty: 18, 38
Andy Hayt/NBAE/Getty: 30
Walter Iooss, Jr./NBAE/Getty: 37
Streeter Lecka/Getty: 16
Wilfredo Lee/AP: 22
Fernando Medina/NBAE/Getty: 34
Eliot J. Schechter/Getty: 4
Gregory Smith/AP: 5, 12
Sports Gallery: 23
Nick Wass/AP: 1, 40, 41
Kathy Willens/AP: 13

**LIBRARY OF CONGRESS
CATALOGING-IN-PUBLICATION DATA**
Gigliotti, Jim.
  The Southeast Division / by Jim Gigliotti and
Robert E. Schnakenberg.
    p. cm. — (Above the rim)
  Includes index.
  ISBN 1-59296-558-X (library bound : alk. paper)
1. National Basketball Association—History—Juvenile
literature. 2. Basketball—Southern states—History—
Juvenile literature. I. Schnakenberg, Robert. II. Title.
III. Series.
  GV885.515.N37G547 2006
  796.323'64'0973—dc22
    2005026208

TABLE OF CONTENTS

INTRODUCTION

When the National Basketball Association (NBA) added the Charlotte Bobcats as its 30th franchise in the 2004–05 season, it also underwent a major **realignment.** Instead of having four divisions of seven or eight teams, the league expanded to six divisions, each with five teams, for the first time.

Guard Dwyane Wade (No. 3) and center Shaquille O'Neal helped carry the Heat to the first Southeast Division championship in 2004–05.

**The Hawks and the Bobcats represent the oldest and
newest NBA franchises in the division.**

One of the new kids on the block was the Southeast Division,
which became a blend of some of the youngest and oldest franchises in the league. Charlotte was placed in the Southeast, along
with other relative NBA newcomers such as the Miami Heat and the

Orlando Magic, both founded in the late 1980s. But those clubs were joined by the Atlanta Hawks, who entered the NBA in its **formative** years in the late 1940s, and the Washington Wizards, who began play while the young league still was gaining a foothold in the American sports scene in the early 1960s.

There wasn't much suspense in the division's first season, when the powerful Miami Heat went 59–23 during the regular season and ran away from their opponents to win the division by 14 games. But with rapidly improving franchises in Washington, Orlando, and Charlotte, along with a proud club with a rich history in Atlanta—and the natural geographic rivalries created by the grouping—you can be sure that the Southeast Division will feature some exciting and competitive races in the coming seasons. This division is one to watch.

Team	Year Founded	Home Arena	Year Arena Opened	Team Colors
Atlanta Hawks	1946	Philips Arena	1999	Red, black, yellow, white, and gold
Charlotte Bobcats	2004	New Charlotte Arena	2005	Orange, blue, silver, and black
Miami Heat	1988	American Airlines Arena	2000	Red, yellow, black, and white
Orlando Magic	1989	TD Waterhouse Centre	1989	Blue, silver, and black
Washington Wizards	1961	MCI Center	1997	Blue, black, and bronze

CHAPTER ONE

THE ATLANTA HAWKS

The franchise originally was based in St. Louis and known as the Blackhawks.

The Atlanta Hawks are one of the NBA's oldest and most historic franchises. That might surprise some people, because the team has only been playing in its current home city since 1968. But the Hawks' basketball tradition stretches back much further than that.

From 1946 to 1951, the team was known as the Tri-City Blackhawks. They played in the old National Basketball League

The Tri-City Blackhawks were named for the three midwestern cities they called home: Moline, Illinois; Rock Island, Illinois; and Davenport, Iowa.

(NBL). In 1949, the NBL merged with another league to form the NBA. One of the team's coaches in these early days was Arnold "Red" Auerbach, who later became the coach of the Boston Celtics.

In 1951, the Blackhawks moved to Milwaukee and shortened their name to the Hawks. Four years later, they moved again—this time to St. Louis. The St. Louis Hawks made the **NBA Finals** in 1957, 1958,

The Hawks were an NBA power in the late 1950s and early 1960s, when they reached the NBA Finals four times in five seasons.

Bob Pettit soared for the Hawks in the 1950s.

1960, and 1961. In 1958, they won it all, defeating Auerbach's Celtics in six games. Leading the Hawks during this period was Bob Pettit, a talented scorer who spent his entire career with the team.

In 1968, the Hawks shocked their fans again

The Hawks' Bob Pettit was named the NBA's first MVP in 1956.

High-flying Dominique Wilkins is the Hawks' all-time leading scorer.

by moving to Atlanta. The modern era of Hawks basketball had begun. The 1970s was an up-and-down decade for the franchise. Highly successful seasons were often followed by disastrous ones. In 1977, millionaire broadcaster Ted Turner bought the team. He helped bring consistency back to the Hawks, laying the groundwork for Central Division titles in 1980 and 1987.

Turner's biggest move came in 1982, when he traded two players to Utah for the rights to Dominique Wilkins, a former All-American player at the University of Georgia. Wilkins led the Hawks through the 1980s. He became the team's all-time leader in both scoring and steals. While the Hawks never won an NBA title during this period, they were one of the league's most entertaining teams.

That trend continued in the 1990s. The Hawks made the playoffs seven straight seasons beginning in 1992–93, and they captured the Central Division crown in 1993–94. They equaled a franchise record that year by winning 57 games during the regular season under coach Lenny Wilkens.

Key players during this run included Wilkins (who was traded

Dominique Wilkins's high-flying exploits earned him a unique nickname: the Human Highlight Film.

Al Harrington led the Hawks in both scoring (17.5 points per game) and rebounding (7.0) in 2004–05.

Lenny Wilkens is a member of the Hall of Fame as both a player and a coach. He played for the St. Louis Hawks from 1960–61 through 1967–68 and coached the Atlanta Hawks from 1993–94 through 1999–2000.

in 1994), center Dikembe Mutombo, and backcourt man Steve Smith. In recent years, the Hawks have not been successful, missing out on the playoffs six consecutive seasons beginning in 1999–2000. They hit rock bottom in 2004–05, winning only 13 games—a franchise low and the poorest mark in the NBA that season.

So Atlanta has begun building its team around younger players such as forwards Al Harrington and Josh Smith and guard Josh Childress. The club also selected former North Carolina forward Marvin Williams with the No. 2 overall pick in the 2005 draft, and acquired veteran guard Joe Johnson. Johnson averaged 17.1 points per game for Phoenix, which won 62 regular-season games in 2004-05.

Given the eventful history of this franchise, it seems like just a matter of time before the Hawks are flying again.

Marvin Williams posed with NBA commissioner David Stern after the Hawks selected the former North Carolina forward with the second pick of the 2005 draft.

In December 2002, Robert L. Johnson became the first African American
majority owner of a major professional sports franchise.

North Carolina fans long have been fanatical about their
college basketball, but the region was left without an NBA
team after the Hornets packed up from Charlotte and moved to New
Orleans following the 2001–02 season. It didn't take long for the
league to move a new club into the area, though. In December 2002,
the NBA awarded an **expansion franchise** to businessman Robert L.

NBA veteran Bernie Bickerstaff became the Bobcats' first coach.

Johnson to begin play in Charlotte in the 2004–05 season.

One of Johnson's first decisions was one of his most important: he hired veteran NBA coach and executive Bernie Bickerstaff as the new club's head coach and general manager. Bickerstaff was hired a full year before the Bobcats were scheduled to take the floor, and he spent the 2003–04 season scouting future opponents and potential players.

Then in June 2004, Bickerstaff engineered a trade that moved the Bobcats up two spots in the NBA draft

Owner Robert L. Johnson, who founded Black Entertainment Television (BET), is on the board of directors or the board of governors of several businesses and organizations, including the Rock and Roll Hall of Fame in Cleveland.

One of the highlights of the Bobcats' first season
was an upset of the division-champion Heat.

to number two overall. With the pick, Charlotte selected former University of Connecticut power forward Emeka Okafor. The rookie, who helped the Huskies win college basketball's national championship his final year in school, would become the franchise's first star.

Once the initial season began, it didn't take long for the Bobcats to register their first victory. In just their second game, Charlotte beat Orlando 111–100—then presented Johnson with the game ball.

As expected for most expansion teams, wins were hard to come by for the Bobcats that first season. But they managed 18 victories, and their youth and enthusiasm resulted in crowd-pleasing efforts throughout the year. Charlotte's most memorable victory was a 94–92 upset over the Heat late in March that was Miami's only loss of the season to a division foe. The Bobcats also recorded two nail-biting victories over Houston in a five-day span in December, and

After the Bobcats selected Emeka Okafor with the second pick of the 2004 draft, the Chicago Bulls took guard Ben Gordon, his former Connecticut teammate, with the third choice.

Before joining Charlotte, Bernie Bickerstaff had coached 11 seasons in the NBA for Seattle, Denver, and Washington.

Center Primoz Brezec averaged 13.0 points per game in the Bobcats' inaugural season.

The Bobcats lost their debut game 103–96 to the Washington Wizards, thanks to the 24 points scored by Antawn Jamison—a one-time resident of North Carolina.

they beat defending league champion Detroit twice, including a 97–86 victory in the final game of the regular season.

Okafor led the club by averaging 15.1 points and 10.9 rebounds per game and was named the league's Rookie of the Year. Other young stars included Primoz Brezec, a 7-foot-1 center from Slovenia who was selected off Indiana's roster in the expansion draft and averaged

Former Connecticut All-American Emeka Okafor is the Bobcats' first big star.

**Guard Brevin Knight helped provide the young Bobcats
with a veteran presence in 2004–05.**

13.0 points and 7.4 rebounds per game; forward Gerald
Wallace, who averaged 11.1 points; and guard Brevin
Knight, who averaged 10.1 points and dished out 9.0
assists per game.

With those players, plus 2005 draftees such as
point guard Raymond Felton and forward Sean May,
the Bobcats figure to become an NBA force sooner
rather than later.

CHAPTER THREE

THE MIAMI HEAT

T he Heat had an **inauspicious** start as an expansion team in the late 1980s. By the 1990s, however, they had emerged as perennial playoff contenders. The Heat's surge to the top of their division coincided with the arrival of Pat Riley as the club's president and head coach in 1995.

Miami joined the league in 1988–89 and began play under coach Ron Rothstein as a member of the Midwest Division. Like most expansion teams, the club struggled early. The Heat, however, took a first-year team's troubles to new heights—or depths. Miami set an NBA record by losing its first 17 games. The club finally ended the drought with an 89–88 victory over the Los Angeles Clippers for its first win.

The Heat won only 15 games that first season. They shifted divisions the next year, joining the Atlantic. The change did little good, as Miami won only 18 games in 1989–1990. The addition of rookie Glen Rice to a roster of returning players such as center Rony Seikaly and forward Grant Long would bode well for the future, however.

By 1991–92, the Heat were in the playoffs, albeit with a losing record (38–44), but they were bounced in the first round by the Chicago Bulls. Two years later, Miami posted its first winning season (42–40) but fell to the Hawks in the first round of the playoffs.

The Heat won 14 consecutive road games in 1996–97. It was the third-longest winning streak away from home in NBA history.

Riley was hired before the 1995–96 season. He had forged his coaching reputation by winning four NBA titles with the Los Angeles Lakers. Riley had never missed the playoffs in 13 seasons with the Lakers and the New York Knicks. That streak surely figured to end when he took over a Miami team that went just 32–50 in 1994–95.

Instead, the streak continued. A series of off-season moves brought in center Alonzo Mourning and guard Tim Hardaway and shipped out Rice.

Former Heat coach Pat Riley directs his team from the bench.

Alonzo Mourning has been a dominating defensive player for the Heat.

Mourning led the team in scoring and rebounding while playing a **tenacious** defense. Tough defense was a big part of Riley's teams.

Miami reached the playoffs in each of Riley's first six seasons, giving him an NBA-record 19 teams he coached to the playoffs. The highlight came in

Glen Rice set a club record when he scored 56 points in a victory over the Orlando Magic on April 15, 1995.

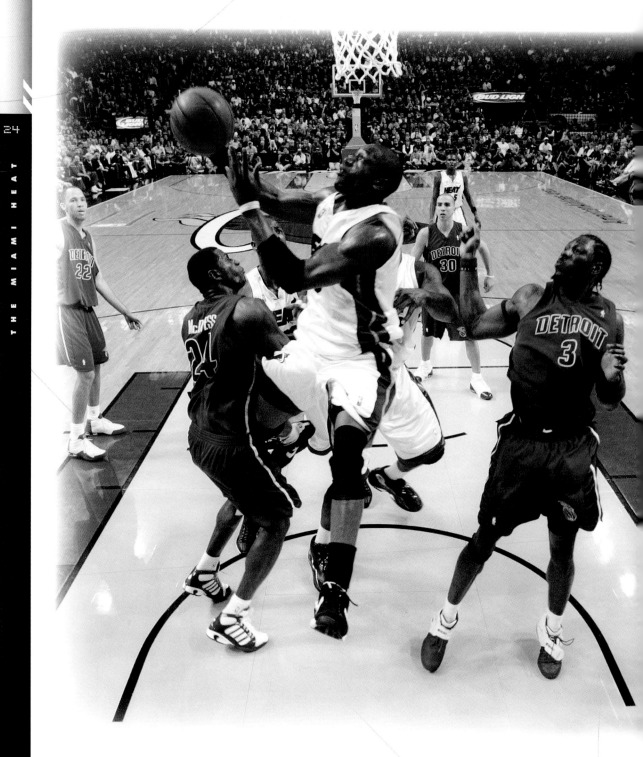

Dwyane Wade has emerged as one of the NBA's top guards.

1996–97, when the Heat posted a franchise-record 61 victories, won the first of four consecutive Atlantic Division titles, and advanced to the Eastern Conference Finals, before losing to Chicago.

The Heat's first-ever draft pick was Syracuse center Rony Seikaly in 1988.

Unfortunately for Miami fans, the Heat could not build on that success in the ensuing seasons, and in 2001–02, the club missed the playoffs for the first time under Riley. Miami's 25–57 record in 2002–03 was its worst since the early days of the franchise, and 2003–04 got off to a rough start when Riley resigned as coach (he stayed on as club president) shortly before the season started. The team opened with seven consecutive losses under new coach Stan Van Gundy.

But help was on the way. First-round draft pick Dwyane Wade, a point guard, became one of the best rookies in the league, and the Heat turned things around to finish 42–40 and make the playoffs.

Hulking center Shaquille O'Neal helped make the Heat instant title contenders.

In August 2005, Miami acquired high-scoring forward Antoine Walker from Boston as part of a 5-team, 13-player deal—the largest in NBA history.

After the season, Miami made huge news by acquiring superstar center Shaquille O'Neal in a trade with the Los Angeles Lakers. O'Neal and Wade gave the Heat a powerful inside-outside combination that led to 59 victories during the 2004–05 regular season. In the playoffs, Miami dispatched New Jersey and Washington with incredible ease, sweeping each series in four games, before running into defending NBA champion Detroit. The Pistons won a dramatic series in seven games to advance to the NBA finals.

It was a banner season for the young franchise. Heat fans hope the best is still to come.

Forward Antoine Walker arrived as part of a blockbuster deal before the 2005–06 season.

CHAPTER FOUR

THE ORLANDO MAGIC

O rlando's meteoric rise from expansion team to NBA finalist in its early years was downright, well . . . magical.

In 1987, owner Jim Hewitt was awarded a franchise for Orlando to begin play in the 1989–1990 season. Former Philadelphia 76ers coach Matt Goukas was picked to lead the first Magic team, which included NBA veterans Reggie Theus and Terry Catledge and rookie Nick Anderson. Orlando only narrowly lost its first game to the New Jersey Nets, then beat the New York Knicks and the Cleveland Cavaliers in its next two games. But the Magic went through an expansion team's typical growing pains, winning just 18 games its first year, 31 the next, and 21 the year after that.

Then a little bit of magic transformed the club overnight. Orlando drew the first pick in the lottery for the 1992 draft and used the choice to select imposing center Shaquille O'Neal from Louisiana State University.

No one knew it at the time, but Orlando had become an instant playoff contender. The Magic improved their victory total by 20 games and finished 41–41 in 1992–93, missing the postseason only by a tiebreaker. O'Neal averaged 23.4 points and 13.9 rebounds and became the first rookie to start in the All-Star Game since Michael Jordan in the mid-1980s.

Illinois forward Nick Anderson was the Magic's first college draft selection (in 1989). He spent 10 seasons with the club and became its all-time leading scorer.

Terry Catledge led the Magic in scoring in their expansion season.

Because Orlando was the best team in the league that didn't make the playoffs in 1992–93, the club had the worst chance of drawing the number-one slot in the 1993 draft lottery. But Orlando's 1-in-66 chance came up, and the club won the drawing.

Hall of Famer Julius Erving joined the Magic front office as executive vice president in 1997.

Guard Anfernee Hardaway teamed with center Shaquille O'Neal
to give the Magic an excellent inside-outside combination.

This time, the Magic selected Michigan forward Chris Webber and then promptly shipped him to the Warriors for guard Anfernee Hardaway. "Penny" was the perfect **complement** to the hulking O'Neal. When Orlando added former Bulls forward Horace Grant to the mix the following year, the team was ready to make a run at the NBA championship.

Orlando's 1994–95 team won 57 games en route to the Atlantic Division title. The Magic then beat Boston, Chicago, and Indiana in the playoffs to reach the NBA Finals in only the franchise's sixth season of existence.

Though the Houston Rockets spoiled Orlando's title hopes, the Magic were now established on the scene. The departure of O'Neal to the Los Angeles Lakers as a **free agent** in 1996 slowed Orlando's momentum, but the club found a new superstar in forward Tracy McGrady, who signed as a free agent in 2000. In 2002–03, McGrady was the league's leading scorer

Magic guard Scott Skiles dished out an NBA record 30 assists in a game against Denver in December 1990.

Tracy McGrady was a prolific scorer who poured in 62 points in this game against Washington in 2004.

(at 32.1 points per game), but the Magic lost in the opening round of the playoffs. He topped the league again the next season at 28.0 points per game, but a disastrous start doomed the club to its first losing season since 1991–92.

That convinced the Magic to head in another direction for 2004–05. McGrady was traded to Houston before the season, and the club began building around veterans such as guard Steve Francis (who was

Steve Francis averaged a team-best 21.3 points per game for the Magic in 2004–05.

Forward Grant Hill jump-started his career again in Orlando.

In 2004, the Magic
drafted forward
Dwight Howard, the
national high school
player of the year.
Then they traded for
former St. Joseph's
guard Jameer
Nelson, who earned
college player of
the year honors that
same year.

acquired in the trade for McGrady) and forward Grant
Hill, and youngsters such as forward Dwight Howard,
the top overall pick of the 2004 draft.

Orlando improved from 21 victories the previous
season to 36 victories in 2004–05, then went back to
the future for 2005–06 by hiring Brian Hill to coach
the team for the second time. Hill was at the helm
when the club forged its best seasons in the mid-
1990s. Orlando fans hope he can bring back that
magic again.

CHAPTER FIVE

THE WASHINGTON WIZARDS

Walt Bellamy (No. 8) was a future Hall of Famer in the early days of the franchise.

Forgive the Washington Wizards if they suffer from a bit of an identity crisis. In a little more than 40 years of existence, they've played under six different names in three different cities.

The Wizards began as the Chicago Packers in 1961–62 and then changed their name to the Chicago Zephyrs the following season. Center Walt Bellamy, the top pick of the 1961 draft and a future Hall of Fame inductee, was the club's first star. But after two uneventful seasons in Chicago produced only 43 victories, a pair of

Former Baltimore Bullets Dave Bing, Elvin Hayes, and Earl Monroe were all inducted into basketball's Hall of Fame in 1990. It's the only time that three members of the same franchise were inducted in the same year.

last-place finishes, and few fans, the franchise moved to Baltimore and became known as the Bullets.

Things soon began looking up. In 1967, the club drafted guard Earl "The Pearl" Monroe from Winston-Salem State. The next year, the Bullets selected center Wes Unseld from the University of Louisville. Along with veterans such as high-flying forward Gus Johnson, the pieces were in place for the most successful period in club history.

The stretch began when the Bullets had their

Wes Unseld (No. 41) was a powerful inside presence.

Washington beat Seattle in the NBA Finals in 1978.

first winning season, going 57–25 in 1968–69. It was the first of 10 winning seasons in 11 years and marked the start of 12 consecutive playoff appearances. Though the 1968–69 team was swept out of the playoffs by New York, the Bullets would reach the NBA Finals four times in the 1970s.

The highlight came in 1977–78, when the franchise won its lone NBA championship. By then, the team had moved to the nation's capital and was

The original Baltimore Bullets lasted from 1947–48 through 1953–54. That franchise won the 1947–48 league title, but it folded before the start of the 1954–55 season.

Not even the incomparable Michael Jordan could lead the Wizards to the playoffs.

known as the Washington Bullets (after being called the Capital Bullets in their first year there), Monroe was playing for the Knicks, and Johnson had retired. Unseld, though, had been joined by 6-foot-9 forward Elvin Hayes, a first-round draft choice in 1968 who was traded to the Bullets in 1972. Hayes would go on to become the franchise's all-time leading scorer. After winning 44 games during the regular season, Washington elimi–nated Atlanta, San Antonio, and Philadelphia in the Eastern Conference playoffs. Then they won a seven-game series over Seattle in the finals.

The SuperSonics avenged their loss to the Bullets in the 1979 finals, and since then, the Bullets have had little success. From 1987–88 to 1995–96, Washington had nine consecutive losing seasons, including three last-place finishes. Before the 1997–98 season, the club changed its name to the Washington Wizards. Little changed on the court, however, and the club gradually declined until it won only 18 games in 1998–99 and 19 games in 2000–01.

Not even the incomparable Michael Jordan could take the Wizards back to the playoffs in the early years of the new millennium. At 38, the former Bulls star came out of retirement to join the Wizards for the 2001–02 season. He led the team by averaging 22.9 points per game and helped Washington improve to 37 victories. But Washington won

Acrobatic forward Gus Johnson reportedly could leap high enough to touch the top of the backboard. He was one of the first players to make a driving slam dunk part of his repertoire.

only 37 games again in 2002–03, narrowly missing
the playoffs, and Jordan retired again.

After another poor season in 2003–04 (only
25 wins and a sixth-place finish in the Atlantic
Division), the Wizards broke through in 2004–05 for
their first playoff appearance since 1996–97. They
improved their win total by a whopping 20 games
behind the stellar play of guards Gilbert Arenas

**Guard Gilbert Arenas and the Wizards celebrated
a long-awaited postseason victory in 2005.**

Antawn Jamison and the Wizards are determined to build on 2004–05's success.

(25.5 points and 5.1 assists per game) and Larry Hughes (22.0 points, 6.3 rebounds, and 4.7 assists), and forward Antawn Jamison (19.6 points and 7.6 rebounds).

In the playoffs, the Wizards beat Chicago for their first win in a postseason series since the early 1980s. Washington's season ended against Miami in the next round, and Hughes soon left the team as a free agent. But the Wizards quickly filled that void by acquiring swingman Caron Butler from the Lakers. Their fans remained hopeful that the year's success meant the franchise had reclaimed its identity—as a winner—once again.

When guard Gilbert Arenas and forward Antawn Jamison each made the Eastern Conference squad in 2004–05, they gave the franchise two All-Stars in the same season for the first time in nearly 18 years.

TIME LINE

1946   The Hawks are founded as the Tri-City Blackhawks

1958   The St. Louis Hawks win the NBA title

1961   The Chicago Packers join the NBA

1963   The Chicago Zephyrs (formerly the Packers) move to Baltimore and become the Bullets

1968   The Hawks move to their current home in Atlanta

1973   The Baltimore Bullets move to Washington and become the Capital Bullets (later the Washington Bullets and now the Washington Wizards)

1978   Washington wins its lone NBA championship

1988   Miami begins play as an expansion team

1989   Orlando begins play as an expansion team

1995   Orlando reaches the NBA Finals in only its sixth season

2004   The Charlotte Bobcats debut as the NBA's 30th team

2005   Miami wins the Southeast in the division's first year of existence

STAT STUFF

TEAM RECORDS

TEAM	ALL-TIME RECORD	NBA TITLES (MOST RECENT)	NUMBER OF TIMES IN PLAYOFFS	TOP COACH (WINS)
Atlanta	2,183–2,237	1 (1957–58)	36	Richie Guerin (327)
Charlotte	18–64	0	0	Bernie Bickerstaff (18)
Miami	660–702	0	10	Pat Riley (354)
Orlando	624–656	0	8	Brian Hill (191)
Washington	1,630–1,935	1 (1977–78)	22	Gene Shue (291)

NBA SOUTHEAST CAREER LEADERS (THROUGH 2004–05)

TEAM	CATEGORY	NAME (YEARS WITH TEAM)	TOTAL
Atlanta	Points	Dominique Wilkins (1982–1994)	23,292
	Rebounds	Kevin Willis (1984–1994)	7,256
Charlotte	Points	Emeka Okafor (2004–05)	1,105
	Rebounds	Emeka Okafor (2004–05)	795
Miami	Points	Glen Rice (1989–1995)	9,248
	Rebounds	Rony Seikaly (1988–1994)	4,544
Orlando	Points	Nick Anderson (1989–1999)	10,650
	Rebounds	Shaquille O'Neal (1992–96)	3,691
Washington	Points	Elvin Hayes (1972–1981)	15,551
	Rebounds	Wes Unseld (1968–1981)	13,769

MORE STAT STUFF

MEMBERS OF THE NAISMITH MEMORIAL NATIONAL
BASKETBALL HALL OF FAME

ATLANTA PLAYER	POSITION	DATE INDUCTED
Red Auerbach	Coach	1969
Walt Bellamy	Center	1993
Walter Brown	Contributor	2005
Clifford Hagan	Guard/Forward	1978
Alex Hannum	Coach	1998
Connie Hawkins	Forward	1992
Red Holzman	Coach	1986
Bob Houbregs	Forward/Center	1987
Clyde Lovellette	Center	1988
Bobby McDermott	Guard	1988
Ed Macauley	Forward/Center	1960
Moses Malone	Center	2001
Pete Maravich	Guard	1987
Slater "Dugie" Martin	Guard	1982
Bob Pettit	Forward/Center	1971
Andy Phillip	Coach	1961
Lenny Wilkens	Guard/Coach	1989

WASHINGTON PLAYER	POSITION	DATE INDUCTED
Walt Bellamy	Center	1993
Dave Bing	Guard	1990
Elvin Hayes	Forward	1990
Bailey Howell	Forward	1997
Moses Malone	Center	2001
Earl Monroe	Guard	1990
Wes Unseld	Center	1988

Note: Charlotte, Miami, and Orlando do not have any members of the Hall of Fame (yet!).

Elvin Hayes was inducted into the Hall of Fame in 1990.

complement—one part that makes another part or parts whole

expansion franchise—a new team that starts from scratch

formative—an early period of growth or development

free agent—an athlete who has finished his contract with one team and is eligible to sign with another

inaugural—the first one

inauspicious—not successful or fortunate

NBA Finals—a seven-game series between the winners of the NBA's Eastern and Western Conference championships

realignment—a change in the way something is organized

repertoire—list or array of skills

tenacious—persistent, not giving up or letting go

FOR MORE INFORMATION ABOUT
THE SOUTHEAST DIVISION AND THE NBA

BOOKS

Bernstein, Ross. *Shaquille O'Neal.* Minneapolis: LernerSports, 2005.

Frisch, Aaron. *The History of the Washington Wizards.* Mankato, Minn.:
Creative Education, 2002.

Gentile, Derek. *Smooth Moves: Juking, Jamming, Hooking & Slamming:
Basketball's Players, Action & Style.* New York: Black Dog &
Leventhal Publishers, 2003.

Hareas, John. *Basketball.* New York: DK Publishers, 2005.

Hudson, David L. *Basketball's Most Wanted II: The Top 10 Book of
More Hotshot Hoopsters, Double Dribbles, and Roundball Oddities.*
Washington, D.C.: Potomac Books, Inc., 2005.

Mandell, Judith. *Super Sports Star Alonzo Mourning.* Berkeley Heights,
N.J.: Enslow Publishers, 2001.

Nichols, John. *The History of the Atlanta Hawks.* Mankato, Minn.:
Creative Education, 2002.

Nichols, John. *The History of the Miami Heat.* Mankato, Minn.:
Creative Education, 2002.

Nichols, John. *The History of the Orlando Magic.* Mankato, Minn.:
Creative Education, 2002.

Owens, Tom. *Basketball Arenas.* Brookfield, Conn.: Millbrook Press,
2002.

ON THE WEB

Visit our home page for lots of links
about The Southeast Division teams:
http://www.childsworld.com/links

Note to Parents, Teachers, and Librarians: We routinely verify our Web links to make
sure they are safe, active sites—so encourage your readers to check them out!

INDEX

ABOUT THE AUTHORS

Jim Gigliotti is a former editor at the National Football League who now is a freelance writer based in Southern California. His writing credits include *Baseball: A Celebration* (with James Buckley Jr.) and *Stadium Stories: USC Trojans*, as well as a dozen children's and young adult books on various sports and personalities.

Robert E. Schnakenberg has written eight books on sports for young readers, including *Teammates: John Stockton and Karl Malone* and *Scottie Pippen: Reluctant Superstar*. He lives in Brooklyn, New York.